Politik und Wirtschaft – bilingual

Topics in European Politics

bearbeitet von:
Udo Hagedorn und
Michael Plügge

C.C.Buchner Verlag · Bamberg

Wirtschaft und Politik – bilingual

Topics in European Politics

Bearbeitet von Udo Hagedorn und Michael Plügge

Zu diesem Lehrwerk sind erhältlich:
- Erwartungshorizonte zu den Aufgaben zum Download auf www.ccbuchner.de (BN 710512)

1. Auflage, 1. Druck 2015
Alle Drucke dieser Auflage sind, weil untereinander unverändert, nebeneinander benutzbar.

Dieses Werk folgt der reformierten Rechtschreibung und Zeichensetzung. Ausnahmen bilden Texte, bei denen künstlerische, philologische oder lizenzrechtliche Gründe einer Änderung entgegenstehen.

Redaktion: Andreas Gerster
Grafische Gestaltung: HOCHVIER GmbH & Co. KG, Bamberg
Druck und Bindung: Friedrich Pustet, Regensburg

www.ccbuchner.de

ISBN 978-3-661-71051-8

Vorwort

Der bilinguale Unterricht hat in den letzten Jahren immer größere Bedeutung gewonnen. Er wird in Form von Modulen oder als durchgehender Sachfachunterricht in einer Fremdsprache erteilt und soll Schülerinnen und Schüler dazu befähigen, fachspezifische Lernbereiche in der Fremdsprache zu erschließen, darzustellen und darüber zu diskutieren. Dadurch erhöht sich die Sprachkompetenz nachhaltig. Da der Sachgegenstand meist aus der Perspektive eines Partnerlandes beleuchtet wird, eignet sich der bilinguale Unterricht auch in besonderem Maße zum Erwerb interkultureller Kompetenzen – eine wichtige Voraussetzung für das Bestehen in einem sprachlich und kulturell vielfältigen Europa und einer global vernetzten Welt.

Mit unserer neuen Reihe **„Politik und Wirtschaft – bilingual“** reagieren wir auf diese Entwicklung und bieten Ihnen thematisch abgeschlossene Module in englischer Sprache, die Sie flexibel im Unterricht einsetzen können. Durch seine vielfältigen internationalen Bezüge und seine kontroversen Themen eignet sich der Politik- und Wirtschaftsunterricht naturgemäß in besonderer Weise für den bilingualen Unterricht – und kann gleichzeitig zu einem wichtigen Baustein bei der Vorbereitung auf eine zunehmend international geprägte Arbeitswelt werden.

Das vorliegende Arbeitsheft **„Topics in European Politics“** eignet sich für den Einsatz in den höheren Jahrgangsstufen der Sekundarstufe I und in der Sekundarstufe II. Es beleuchtet verschiedene Aspekte des Themenfeldes Europäische Union, wie z. B. Migration, Binnenmarkt, Eurokrise und Nationalismus. Dabei wird an vielen Stellen auf die besondere Perspektive Großbritanniens und dessen spannungsreiches und ungeklärtes Verhältnis zur Europäischen Integration eingegangen.

Die Konzeption des Heftes erschließt sich leicht:

- Jedes Unterkapitel enthält eine Sammlung interessanter Materialien und Texte, die mit Hilfe eines Aufgabenapparates („Exercises“) erschlossen werden können.
- In der Randspalte befinden sich Begriffserläuterungen und Hinweise auf weiterführende Informationen.
- Der Serviceteil enthält einen Vokabelteil zu den Materialien und eine Sammlung nützlicher Redemittel für die Diskussion in der Klasse.

Das Autorenteam wünscht Ihnen fruchtbare Diskussionen und spannende neue Einsichten in den vielschichtigen Prozess der Europäischen Einigung!

TABLE OF CONTENTS

Table of Contents

1. Getting closer to the EU

1.1 What do you know about the EU?

M 1 Countries and candidates of the EU

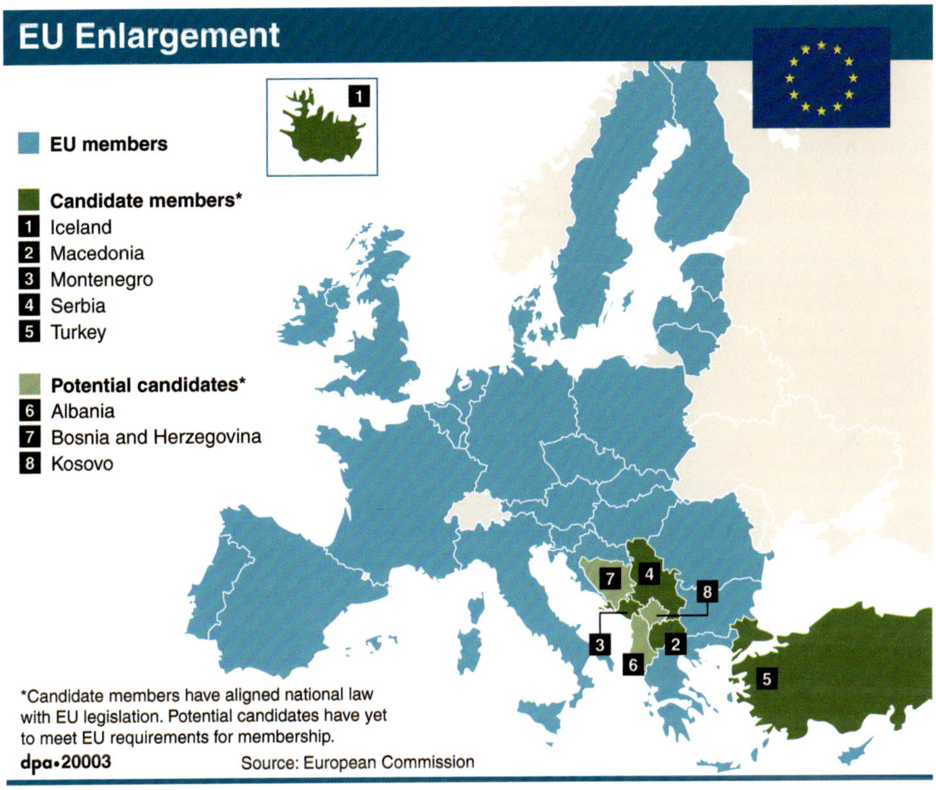

The EU was not always as big as it is today. When European countries started to co-operate economically in 1951, only Belgium, Germany, France, Italy, Luxembourg and the Netherlands participated. Over time, more and more countries decided to join. The union reached its current size of 28 member countries with the accession of Croatia on the 1st of July 2013.

Exercises

1. Form groups of 4 students and create a poster that illustrates everything you know about the "EU". Include a wide variety of topics, such as concepts, hopes, and fears related to the EU.
2. Work with a partner. You may use the Internet, if necessary.
   - Identify the countries on the map of Europe and name their capitals.
   - Name the language(s) spoken in each of the countries.
   - Find out the name of the nationality of each country (e.g. Germany > Germans).
   - List the countries in which the Euro is used as the official currency.

M 2 Quiz concerning the EU

Tick the correct answers (sometimes more than one can be correct).

1. How many gold stars are there on the EU flag?
   - o 10
   - o 11
   - o 12
   - o 13

2. What colour is the 20 EUR note?
   - o Red
   - o Blue
   - o Green
   - o Orange

3. The Treaty of Rome, which established the EEC (forerunner of the EU) was signed in what year?
   - o 1949
   - o 1953
   - o 1957
   - o 1961

4. How many countries signed the Treaty of Rome and consequently became the first countries of the EEC?
   - o 4
   - o 5
   - o 6
   - o 7

5. Name the port city situated at the mouth of the river Rhine.
   - o Rotterdam
   - o Amsterdam
   - o Hamburg
   - o The Hague

6. In which city is the International Court of Justice?
   - o Brussels
   - o The Hague
   - o Strasbourg
   - o Luxembourg

7. On which sea are Latvia and Lithuania situated?
   - o North Sea
   - o East Sea
   - o Baltic Sea
   - o Black Sea

8. The Canary Islands are part of which country?
   - o Portugal
   - o Spain
   - o France
   - o Italy

9. In which country was LEGO invented ?
   - o Sweden
   - o Norway
   - o Finland
   - o Denmark

10. Which EU countries flag features the map of the country?
    - o Malta
    - o Cyprus
    - o Bulgaria
    - o Latvia

11. On what date each year is "Europe Day" celebrated?
    - o 1st of May
    - o 9th of May
    - o 17th of June
    - o 1st of November

12. Who composed the Ninth Symphony that includes 'Ode to Joy', the European Anthem?
    - o Bach
    - o Mozart
    - o Schubert
    - o Beethoven

13. How many member states are in the EU at present?
    - o 26
    - o 27
    - o 28
    - o 29

14. What two countries became part of the EU in 2007?
    - o Slovenia
    - o Romania
    - o Bulgaria
    - o Croatia

15. In which city is the European Commission based?
    - o The Hague
    - o Brussels
    - o Luxembourg
    - o Frankfurt

16. Which city had the first underground rail system?
    - o London
    - o Paris
    - o Madrid
    - o Berlin

17. In which year did the Euro notes and coins come into general use?
    - o 2000
    - o 2001
    - o 2002
    - o 2003

18. In which year did a group of 10 additional countries join the EU?
    - o 2004
    - o 2005
    - o 2006
    - o 2007

19. Which is the smallest EU country?
    - o Cyprus
    - o Denmark
    - o Malta
    - o Portugal

20. Which country joined the EU in 2004 and has a coastline on the Adriatic Sea?
    - o Croatia
    - o Slovakia
    - o Slovenia
    - o Italy

Quelle (Auszüge): http://www.euireland.ie/europack/assets/pdf/Europack.pdf (10.7.2014)

Key: 1: 12; 2: blue; 3: 1957; 4: 6; 5: Rotterdam; 6: The Hague; 7: Baltic; 8: Spain; 9: Denmark; 10: Cyprus; 11: 9th of May; 12: Beethoven; 13: 28; 14: Romania/Bulgaria; 15: Brussels; 16: London; 17: 2002; 18: 2004; 19: Malta; 20: Slovenia

1.2 The History of the EU

M 3 The Founding Fathers of the EU

The visionary leaders in the picture below inspired the creation of the European Union, in which we live today. Without their energy and motivation we would not be living in the peaceful and stable world that we take for granted. From resistance fighters to lawyers, the founding fathers were a diverse group of people who held the same ideals: a peaceful, united and prosperous Europe. In addiction to the founding fathers listed below, many others have worked tirelessly towards the European project and have inspired it in their own way. This section concerning the founding fathers of the EU is therefore a work in progress.

Konrad Adenauer | Winston Churchill | Alcide De Gasperi | Walter Hallstein | Jean Monnet | Robert Schuman

M 4 Winston Churchill's dream of a united Europe

Churchill addresses The Congress of Europe May 7, 1948, The Hague

Since I spoke on this subject at Zurich in 1946, and since our British United Europe Movement was launched in January 1947, events have carried our affairs beyond our expectations. This cause was obviously either vital or merely academic. If it was academic, it would wither by the wayside; but if it were the vital need of Europe and the world in this dark hour, then the spark would start a fire which would glow brighter and stronger in the hearts and the minds of men and women in many lands.
This is what has actually happened. Great governments have banded themselves together with all their executive power. The mighty republic of the United States has espoused the Marshall Plan. Sixteen European States are now associated for economic purposes; five have entered into close economic and military relationship. We hope that this nucleus will in due course be joined by the peoples of Scandinavia, and of the Iberian peninsula, as well as by Italy, who should now resume her full place in the comity of nations. [...]
This is not a movement of parties but a movement of peoples. There is no room for jealousies. If there is rivalry of parties, let it be to see which one will distinguish itself the most for the common cause. No one can suppose that Europe can be united on any party or sectional basis, any more than any one nation can assert an overweening predominance. It must be all for all. Europe can only be united by the heart-felt wish and vehement expression of the great majority of all the peoples in all the parties in all the freedom-loving countries, no matter where they dwell or how they vote. [...]

Winston Churchill

Sir Winston Leonard Spencer-Churchill (1874–1965) was a British politician. He was the Prime Minister of the United Kingdom from 1940 to 1945 and again from 1951 to 1955. Widely regarded as one of the greatest wartime leaders of the 20th century, Churchill was also an officer in the British Army, a historian, a writer (under the pen name Winston S. Churchill), and an artist.

The Movement for European Unity must be a positive force, deriving its strength from our sense of common spiritual values. It is a dynamic expression of democratic faith based upon moral conceptions and inspired by a sense of mission. In the centre of our movement stands the idea of a Charter of Human Rights, guarded by freedom and sustained by law. [...]
Some time ago I stated that it was the proud mission of the victor nations to take the Germans by the hand and lead them back into the European family, and I rejoice that some of the most eminent and powerful Frenchmen have spoken in this sense. To rebuild Europe from its ruins and make its light shine forth again upon the world, we must first of all conquer ourselves. It is in this way only that the sublime, with its marvellous transmutations of material things, can be brought into our daily life. Europe requires all that Frenchmen, all that Germans, and all that every one of us can give. I therefore welcome here the German delegation, whom we have invited into our midst. For us the German problem is to restore the economic life of Germany and revive the ancient fame of the German race without thereby exposing their neighbours and ourselves to any rebuilding or reassertion of their military power of which we still bear the scars. United Europe provides the only solution to this two-sided problem and is also a solution which can be implemented without delay.

http://www.churchill-society-london.org.uk/WSCHague.html (12.6.2014)

M 5 ● Past Decades – the Evolution of the European Union

1945 – 1959

A peaceful Europe – the beginnings of cooperation
The European Union is established with the aim of ending the frequent and bloody wars between neighbours, which culminated in the Second World War. As of 1950, the European Coal and Steel Community begins to unite European countries economically and politically in order to secure lasting peace. The six founding countries are Belgium, France, Germany, Italy, Luxembourg and the Netherlands. The 1950s are dominated by a cold war between east and west. In 1957, the Treaty of Rome established the European Economic Community (EEC), or 'Common Market'.

1960 – 1969

The 'Swinging Sixties' – a period of economic growth
It is a period of economic growth, helped by the fact that EU countries stop charging custom duties when they trade with one another. They also agree to take joint control over food production, so that everyone has enough to eat – and soon there is even a surplus of agricultural produce. May 1968 becomes famous for student riots in Paris, and many changes in society and behaviour become associated with the so-called '68 generation'.

1970 – 1979

A growing community – the first enlargement
Denmark, Ireland and the United Kingdom join the European Union on 1 January 1973, raising the number of member states to nine. The Arab-Israeli war of October 1973 results in an energy crisis and economic problems in Europe. The last right-wing dictatorships of Europe come to an end with the overthrow of the Salazar regime in Portugal in 1974 and the death of Spains's General Franco in 1975. The EU's regional policy is implemented and huge sums are transferred to poorer areas in order to create jobs and develop infrastructure. The European Parliament increases its influence in EU affairs and in 1979 all citizens can, for the first time, elect their members directly.

1980 – 1989

The changing face of Europe – the fall of the Berlin Wall
The Polish trade union, Solidarność, and its leader Lech Walesa, become household names across Europe and the world following the Gdansk shipyard strikes in the summer of 1980. In 1981, Greece becomes the 10th member of the EU and Spain and Portugal follow five years later. In 1986 the Single European Act is signed. This treaty provides the basis for a vast six-year programme aimed at solving the problems resulting from the free-flow of trade across EU borders. It creates the 'Single Market'. On 9 November 1989, the fall of the Berlin Wall causes major political upheaval as the border between East and West Germany is opened for the first time in 28 years. This event led to the reunification of Germany in October 1990.

1990 – 1999

A Europe without frontiers
With the collapse of communism across central and Eastern Europe, Europeans become closer neighbours. In 1993 the implementation of the Single Market is completed guaranteeing the 'four freedoms': freedom of movement of goods, of services, of people and of money. The 1990s are also the decade of two treaties, the 'Maastricht' Treaty on the European Union in 1993, and the Treaty of Amsterdam in 1999. People are concerned about environmental issues and about the way in which Europeans can cooperate in terms of security and defence matters. In 1995 the EU gains three new members, Austria, Finland and Sweden. A small village in Luxembourg gives its name to the 'Schengen' Agreements which gradually allow European citizens to travel without having their passports checked at the borders. Millions of young people are able to go study in other countries thanks to the support of the EU. Communication is made easier as more and more people start to use mobile phones and the internet.

2000 – 2009

Further expansion
The Euro becomes the new currency for many Europeans. 11 September 2001 becomes synonymous with the 'War on Terror' after hijacked airliners are flown into buildings in New York and Washington. EU countries begin to work together more closely in order to fight crime. The political divisions between east and west Europe are finally declared healed when no fewer than 10 new countries join the EU in 2004, followed by two more in 2007. A financial crisis hits the global economy in September 2008, resulting in closer economic cooperation between EU countries. The Treaty of Lisbon is ratified by all EU countries before entering into force on 1 December 2009. It provides the EU with modern institutions and more efficient working methods.

2010 – today

A decade of opportunities and challenges
The new decade starts with a severe economic crisis, but also with the hope that investments in new green and climate-friendly technologies and closer European cooperation will bring lasting growth and welfare.

http://europa.eu/geninfo/legal_notices_de.htm, © Europäische Union, 1995 – 2014

Exercises

1. Have a closer look at the founding fathers of the EU (M 3). What kind of people were they, where did they come from and what were their motifs? The exercise can be done in groups or in form of oral presentations.
2. Summarise Churchill's main ideas concerning the necessity of forming a united Europe (M 4).
3. Illustrate the idea of 'European Unity' on a large poster (M 4, M 5).

M 6 ● Europa and the bull

Curt Stenvert (1987), Europa and the bull; Airport Restaurant, Düsseldorf

M 7 ● The role of EU treaties

The complete texts of treaties, legislation, case law and legislative proposals can be read on: *http://eur-lex.europa.eu/collection/eu-laws/treaties.html*

The European Union is based on the rule of law. Every action taken by the EU is founded on treaties that have been approved voluntarily and democratically by all EU member countries. For example, if a policy area is not cited in a treaty, the Commission cannot propose a law in that area. A treaty is a binding agreement between EU member countries. It sets out EU objectives, clarifies rules for EU institutions, determines how decisions are made and what relationships bind the EU and its member countries. Treaties are amended to make the EU more efficient and transparent, to prepare for new member countries and to introduce new areas of cooperation – such as the single currency. Under the treaties, EU institutions can adopt legislations, which the member countries then implement.

The main treaties are:

Treaty of Lisbon	
Signed: 13 December 2007	**Entered into force:** 1 December 2009
Purpose	To make the EU more democratic, more efficient and better able to address global problems, such as climate change, with one voice.
Main changes	More power for the European Parliament, change of voting procedures in the Council, citizens' initiative, a permanent president of the European Council, a new High Representative for Foreign Affairs, a new EU diplomatic service. The Lisbon treaty clarifies which powers: • belong to the EU • belong to EU member countries • are shared.
Comment: The Treaty establishing a constitution for Europe (2004) – with aims similar to the Lisbon Treaty – was signed but never ratified.	

Treaty of Nice	
Signed: 26 February 2001	**Entered into force:** 1 February 2003
Purpose	To reform the institutions so that the EU could function efficiently after reaching 25 member countries.
Main changes	Methods for changing the composition of the Commission and redefining the voting system in the Council.

Treaty of Amsterdam	
Signed: 2 October 1997	**Entered into force:** 1 May 1999
Purpose	To reform EU institutions in preparation for the arrival of future member countries.
Main changes	Amendment, renumbering and consolidation of EU and EEC treaties. More transparent decision-making (increased use of the co-decision voting procedure).

Treaty on European Union – Maastricht Treaty	
Signed: 7 February 1992	**Entered into force:** 1 November 1993
Purpose	To prepare for the European Monetary Union and to introduce elements of a political union (citizenship, common foreign and internal affairs policy).
Main changes	Establishment of the European Union and introduction of the co-decision procedure, giving Parliament more say in decision-making. New forms of cooperation between EU governments – for example on defence, justice and home affairs.

Single European Act	
Signed: 17 February 1986 (Luxembourg)/ 28 February 1986 (The Hague)	**Entered into force:** 1 July 1987
Purpose	To reform the institutions in preparation for Portugal and Spain's membership and accelerate decision-making procedures in preparation for the single market.
Main changes	The extension of qualified majority voting in the Council (making it harder for a single country to veto proposed legislation), and the creation of the cooperation and assent procedures, which give Parliament more influence

Treaties of Rome – EEC and EURATOM treaties	
Signed: 25 March 1957	**Entered into force:** 1 January 1958
Purpose	To set up the European Economic Community (EEC) and the European Atomic Energy Community (Euratom).
Main changes	Extension of European integration to include general economic cooperation.

Treaty establishing the European Coal and Steel Community	
Signed: 18 April 1951	**Entered into force:** 23 July 1952 **Expired:** 23 July 2002
Purpose	To create interdependence in the coal and steel industry so that one country could no longer mobilise its armed forces without others knowing. This treaty eased distrust and tensions after WWII. The ECSC treaty expired in 2002.

http://eur-lex.europa.eu, © Europäische Union, 1998 – 2014

M 8 ● The Enlargement of the EU

Whenever new countries join the EU, the founding treaties have to be amended:

1973 Denmark, Ireland, United Kingdom

1981 Greece

1986 Spain, Portugal

1995 Austria, Finland, Sweden

2004 Czech Republic, Cyprus, Estonia, Hungary, Latvia, Lithuania, Malta, Poland, Slovakia, Slovenia

2007 Bulgaria, Romania

2013 Croatia

M 9 ● Joachim Gauck's Speech on the prospects for the European idea

Full Text of Joachim Gauck's Speech: *http://www.bundespraesident.de/SharedDocs/Reden/EN/JoachimGauck/Reden/2013/130222-Europe.html*

Ladies and gentlemen,

Deep in our hearts, we Germans in particular know that there is something that ties us to Europe in a special way.
After all, it was from our country that the attempts to destroy everything European and all universal values were unleashed. Despite everything that happened, the Allies granted our country support and solidarity straight after the war. We were spared what could so easily have followed our hubris: an existence as a disowned outcast outside the family of nations. Instead, we were invited, received and welcomed – something which seems especially unexpected and wonderful from today's viewpoint. We became partners!

We had the fortunate experience of learning to respect ourselves and being respected by others when we wanted to be "not above and not below other peoples". We have committed ourselves to Europe. Indeed, we have pledged ourselves to Europe.

Today we renew this pledge.

We will pause to consider before crossing the threshold, we will rethink the situation. Then armed with new ideas and good reasons, we will renew confidence, strengthen our commitment and continue to build what we have been building – Europe.

Joachim Gauck, Schloss Bellevue, 22 February 2013

Exercises

1. Describe the picture (M 6). Find out what symbolic elements it represents (internet research).
2. Outline how the EU developed in form and content. Additional research may be necessary to gather more detailed information on the various treaties (M 3, M 5, M 7).
3. Find and read the full speech of Mr Gauck, the German President, on the Internet (M 9) and compare it to Churchill's speech cited above. What parallels can you find? How does Mr Gauck build on Churchill's ideas?

1.3 EU institutions and the EU of the people

M 10 ● EU-elections in May 2014 – Headlines

BBC NEWS Europe
Euroskeptic 'earthquake' rocks EU elections

FINANCIAL TIMES
Ukip and FN lead populist earthquake

THE IRISH TIMES
Sharp rise in support for Eurosceptic parties the dominant story across EU
While mainstream parties hold balance of power, protest vote is substantial

The INDEPENDENT
Ukip tops polls in UK. National Front wins in France. Greek neo-Nazis secure first MEPs. This is the day Europe took a swing to the right

Reuters
French far right in 'earthquake' Europe votes

Mirror
Marine Le Pen's Front National rocks Europe after topping Euro polls in France

The Telegraph
Ukip storms European elections, 'terrifying' political establishment

BloombergBusinessweek
NewsFromBloomberg
Bloomberg News
EU Protest Forces Surge Posing Threat From U.K. to Greece

Sky News
Eurosceptic parties shake EU polls

THE HUFFINGTON POST
UNITED KINGDOM
European Elections 2014: German Party Dubbed 'Neo Nazis' Among Far Right Projected To Win Seats

M 11 ● The European Parliament

Shot Across the Bow
Eurosceptic and anti-European parties made big gains in the European Parliament elections.
Vote projections indicate that those parties could get about 140 of 751 seats in the EU legislature.

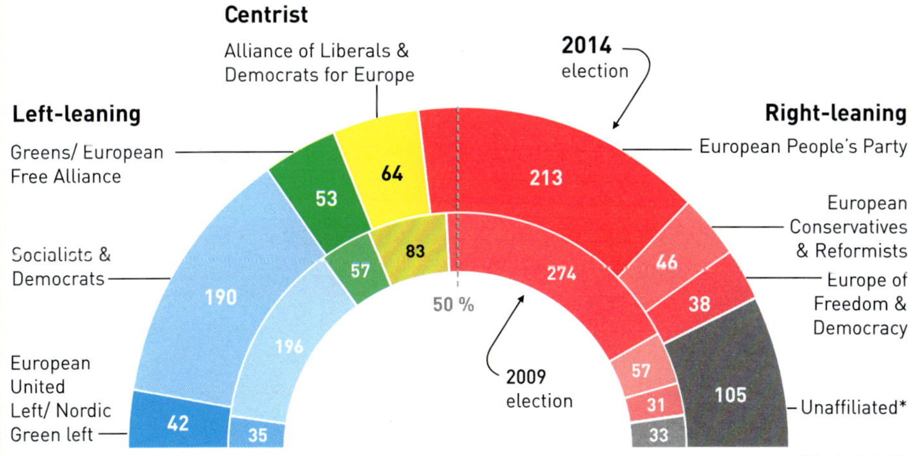

Sources: TNS/ Scyt in cooperation with the European Parliament
*Mostly Anti-EU
The Wall Street Journal

M 12 The EU's institutions

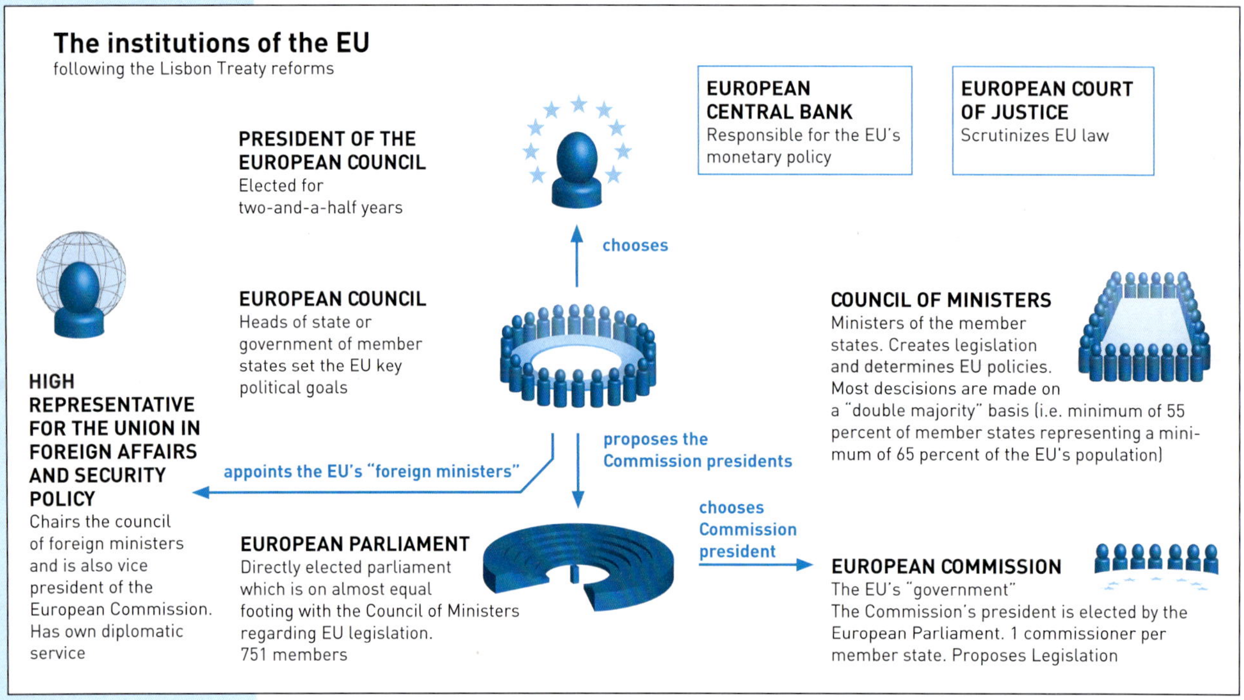

nach: http://www.spiegel.de/international/europe/bild-742565-175282.html (23.7.2014)

On July 1st, 2014 MEPs re-elected Martin Schulz as President of the European Parliament for another two and a half year term. The 58-year old German MEP will lead Parliament until January 2017.

Decision-making at EU level involves various European institutions, including:

- the European Parliament, which represents the EU's citizens and is directly elected by them;
- the European Council, which consists of the Heads of State or Government of the EU Member States;
- the Council, which represents the governments of the EU Member States;
- the European Commission, which represents the interests of the EU as a whole.

The European Council defines the general political direction and priorities of the EU but it does not exercise legislative functions. Generally, it is the European Commission that proposes new laws and it is the European Parliament and Council that adopt them. The Member States and the Commission then implement them.

© European Union, 2013, The European Union explained: How the European Union Works, p. 5

You can find more information about the EU's institutions at:
http://europa.eu/about-eu/institutions-bodies/index_en.htm

M 13 Tony Blair urges EU to elect a president

Tony Blair has called on the European Union to consider carrying out continent-wide elections for a President of Europe, a move he claimed would restore confidence in the wake of the Eurozone crisis.

The former Labour prime minister, who has hinted in the past that he would consider taking the job, said an elected president would help voters feel less alienated from Brussels.

"Out of this European crisis can come the opportunity finally to achieve a model of European integration that is sustainable", Mr Blair told an audience of senior politicians in Berlin. "A Europe-wide election for the presidency of the Commission or Council is the most direct way to involve the public. An election for a big post held by one person – this people can understand."

The proposal was one of a raft of measures that Mr Blair said were necessary to restore the confidence of the public and markets. He added that economic and political reforms of the EU should be implemented as part of a "Grand Bargain", rather than in incremental steps, as has been the case so far. "We should recognise that the underlying, profound rationale for Europe and its union is stronger than ever," he added.

Mr Blair's proposals are likely to be viewed as a further hint that he is positioning himself as a candidate for such a job. In the run-up to the Lisbon Treaty, Mr Blair was tipped as a front-runner for the newly created post of EU President. [...]

"What the people of this country want is not a directly elected president, but a referendum on our future relationship with Europe," he added.

A spokesman for Tony Blair's office said the idea of a directly elected president was „not new at all", and was touted by Mr Blair and other European leaders as early as 2003 "as a way to help close the democratic deficit of the EU".

Richard Hall, The Independent, 29 October 2012

Tony Blair

British Labour Party politican (born 6 May 1953), who served as British Prime Minister from 1994 to 2007.

Exercises

1. In May 2014 the citizen of the EU member states were called to elect the new EU parliament. Have a look at the headlines and statistics in M 10 and M 11 and summarise the main results and outcome of the elections.
2. Discuss: What are the causes behind these results?
3. Explain how the EU works (M 12,). Form groups and prepare short, but detailed presentations on the following institutions with a special focus on their composition and function. You will find detailed information on the official homepage of the EU.
   a. the European Parliament;
   b. the European Council
   c. the Council of the European Union (simply called "the Council");
   d. the European Commission;
   e. the Court of Justice of the European Union;
   f. the European Central Bank;
4. Compare the principles of operation of the EU to the Federal Republic of Germany. Discuss which one offers a higher level of democracy.
5. Watch or read Mr Schulz's acceptance speech and summarise its main points.
6. There are several "presidents" chairing EU institutions. Name them and their functions. What kind of president does former UK Prime Minister Tony Blair have in mind (M 13) and how does this position differ from the others? Why does he ask for the implementation of such a position?

2. The European Union – United or divided?

2.1 Europe in Crisis?

M 1 A boat called EU?

Cartoon: Steve Bell

M 2 Trust in the EU as an institution

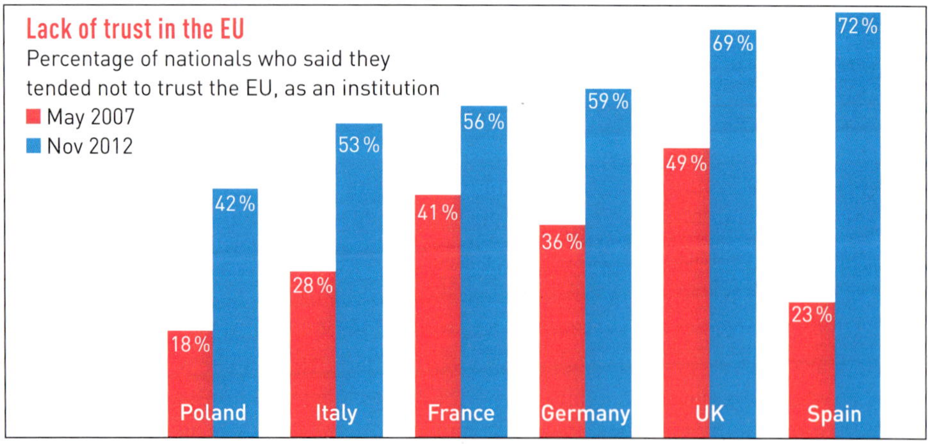

Source: EU, Eurobarometer 2013

M 3 Crisis for Europe as trust hits record low

Public confidence in the European Union has fallen to historically low levels in the six biggest EU countries, raising fundamental questions about its democratic legitimacy more than three years into the union's worst ever crisis, new data shows.
After financial, currency and debt crises, wrenching budget and spending cuts, rich nations' bailouts of the poor, and surrenders of sovereign powers over policymaking to international technocrats, Euroscepticism is soaring to a degree that is likely to feed populist anti-EU politics and frustrate European leaders' efforts to arrest the collapse in support for their project.
Figures from Eurobarometer, the EU's polling organisation, analysed by the European Council on Foreign Relations (ECFR), a thinktank, show a vertiginous decline in trust in the EU in countries such as Spain, Germany and Italy that are historically very pro-European.
The six countries surveyed – Germany, France, Britain, Italy, Spain, and Poland – are the EU's biggest, jointly making up more than two out of three EU citizens or around 350 million of the EU's 500 million population.
The findings, published exclusively in the Guardian in Britain and in collaboration with other leading newspapers in the other five countries, represent a nightmare for Europe's leaders, whether in the wealthy north or in the bailout-battered south, suggesting a much bigger crisis of political and democratic legitimacy.
"The damage is so deep that it does not matter whether you come from a creditor, debtor country, Euro would-be member or the UK: everybody is worse off," said José Ignacio Torreblanca, head of the ECFR's Madrid office. "Citizens now think that their national democracy is being subverted by the way the Euro crisis is conducted."
EU leaders are aware of the problem, utterly at odds over what to do about it, and have yet to come up with any coherent policy proposals addressing the mismatch between the pooling of economic and fiscal powers and the democratic mandate deemed necessary to underpin such radical policy shifts.
José Manuel Barroso, the former European commission president, said European "dream" was under threat from a "resurgence of populism and nationalism" across the EU. "At a time when so many Europeans are faced with unemployment, uncertainty and growing inequality, a sort of 'European fatigue' has set in, coupled with a lack of understanding. Who does what, who decides what, who controls whom and what? And where are we heading to?"

Ian Traynor, The Guardian, 24 April 2013

M 4 Angela Merkel: saviour or tormentor? Europeans give verdict

Efficient, organised and successful. Arrogant, dominant and authoritarian. Saviour of the European project. Merciless tormentor of anyone south of the "olive line". For some, the Eurozone would have collapsed without German leadership. For others, tens of millions of southerners would have been better off without it.
In the runup to German elections this month that will have a crucial bearing on the rest of the continent, the Guardian, Le Monde in France, El País in Spain and La Stampa in Italy asked readers for their view of German leadership in the Euro crisis, as well as of the vote itself. The exercise generated a surprisingly robust response from more than 7,000 readers. Such surveys can never be statistically relevant because of the self-selecting nature of the exercise. But among the jokes and hostility

– and the inevitable rogue entries from people calling themselves things like Ernst Stavro Blofeld and Philip Schleswig-Holstein-Sonderburg-Glücksburg – certain trends were unavoidable.

In the Spanish survey, the overwhelming tone of the response was negative. "Germany is looking to increase its power, imposing solutions that go well in Germany," wrote Alessandro Gimenez. "It's trying to change the southern countries into a cheap workforce, without rights or legal or work security. It perceives the Euro as a single currency when it is convenient to do so and as a confederation of currencies when it is in its interest."

Karen González said Germany had profited from the crisis, abandoned the EU's core principles and had "preferred patching things up than undertaking a true cure at the heart of these problems which are now suffocating countries like Spain, which could backfire".

Germany's insistence on fiscal rigour in return for EU bailout funds had made matters worse in countries crying out for a bit of growth to lessen the pain, many readers opined.

In recent months, the Eurozone crisis has gone into another of its periodic remissions, as government borrowing costs have tracked lower and the continent shows a few delicate signs of economic recovery.

But for Greeks such as Ioannis Pelegrinis, the worst is still to come. "The German leadership is clearly looking out for its own financial interests, as the government of any sovereign country should. Unfortunately, they are doing so at the expense of other EU and Eurozone members. That exactly is the sort of attitude that will bring the dissolution of the EU."

Italians produced a very mixed response, with plenty of criticism tempered by the occasional vote of confidence. "We should be grateful to Germany for the structural changes we've seen in Europe," wrote Lorenzo Iorio. Ezio Dallocchio urged Italians to be more charitable. "They are a model economically and politically for others to copy and not to hate as many of us stupid Italians do."

Northern Europeans were more inclined to give Germans the benefit of the doubt – though many respondents argued that Berlin is acting in its own national interests and not through any broader motivation as a quasi-European leader.

Briton Darren Mills said: "The chancellor and her country have stood steadfast behind their neighbours and EU partners. This is even though the path followed by Germany is not the one that will bring acclamation, or even necessarily benefit. Leadership is not necessarily the art of being 100 % correct, it is the art of being seen to be strong and at the forefront. Germany has shown leadership, more importantly considered leadership."

On the subject of leadership, some respondents argued Germany had demonstrated too much arrogance, while others sensed a reluctance – born of historical precedence – to assume control. All of which left one anonymous respondent to quip: "If you're being criticised from both sides, you've probably found the centre ground."

[...]

As for Merkel, some saw a stubborn control freak acting in her country's interests, while others were more charitable, viewing her as a pragmatist who could see the bigger picture. Dutchwoman Anouk van den Waal argued that: "If there could be an emergency machine that manufactures leaders in a crisis, Mrs Merkel is probably something we would have programmed into it. To Europeans, she doesn't seem to have ideology, she is pragmatic, I don't think many could say if she was left or rightwing. She doesn't take risks, she is quietly strong, she is consensual."

Mark Rice-Oxley, The Guardian, 10 September 2013

M 5 ● Germany's leading role in Europe

Schuck/toonpool.com (15.1.2012)

M 6 ● Something in common: should English be the official language of the EU?

German president Joachim Gauck's cost-cutting proposal has been welcomed – but not by all.

Money talks, especially in Brussels. A billion Euros are usually "mil milhoes de Euros" in Portuguese, or a thousand million. In Spanish, likewise, "billon" means a million million, so billion is "mil millones de Euros". Confusingly, "billion" translates as "milijarde" into Croatian, or "miljard" into Dutch. When the French talk of "un billion", they are referring to what Britons call a trillion. Oh, and a German "Billiarde" is a French "quadrillion". Of course.

Translation in the EU's headquarters is a complicated – and often costly – business. The European commission has three official "procedural languages": German, French and English. But with the Union expanding and 23 languages now spoken in member states, the number of translators has ballooned from 200 – 300 to 2,000 – 3,000. It is estimated that the EU produces 1.76 m pages of translation work a year, costing 300 m (£ 257 m). [...]

In these austere times, national governments are eager to trim the EU budget, which is one reason why a recent speech by the German president was welcomed with such enthusiasm. In a keynote speech on the future of European integration in February, Joachim Gauck suggested English should become the EU's official language: "It is true to say that young people are growing up with English as the lingua franca. However, I feel that we should not simply let things take their course when it comes to linguistic integration." It was music to the ears of federalists and fiscal hawks: with English spoken in the corridors of Brussels, the EU would become more streamlined and more efficient.

But how realistic is it? To an extent, it would just confirm a trend already taking place. Since the "big bang" of eastern European enlargement in 2004, the use of French has declined in conference meetings – and German is these days an "official language" on paper only. Documents in the European parliament are only translated into relevant languages: there are no transcripts on common fisheries policies in Czech, for example.

But if northern and eastern member states would welcome English as an official language, the south would be up in arms. Some French diplomats say English would smuggle "Anglo-Saxon" notions about politics and the economy into the heart of European policymaking. Last December, a journalist from the French daily Libération boycotted a press conference on the EU presidency in Dublin because it was solely in English. If there really was no money for translators, he argued on his blog, it should have been held in Gaelic instead.

There would be legal obstacles too. "Imposing English as the official language of Europe would be profoundly undemocratic," said Diego Marani, a novelist and policy officer for the Directorate-General for Interpretation at the European commission. Far from making Europe more integrated, it could make the project even more elitist. The total cost of EU language work, according to Marani, works out at roughly the cost of two coffees each person each year: a small price to pay for a bit more democracy.

How about alternative solutions? A proposal to make Latin the official working language is sadly an old April fool, but one interpreter thinks Esperanto would be a fairer lingua franca than English. Another suggests a rule whereby diplomats should never be allowed to speak in their mother tongue to create an even playing field. In Marani's office, employees have been experimenting with "Europanto", which he describes as "der jazz des linguas": a freestyle mash-up language made up of the common body of European languages, without grammar rules and an unlimited vocabulary.

Europanto is a joke, of course, but it may carry a serious message. Imposing a common European language may be a political impossibility, but that's not to say that such a language won't develop naturally in the long run anyway. Last year a frustrated senior translator at the European court of auditors compiled a 33-page document on commonly misused English phrases in EU publications ("to precise" meaning "to summarise" for example, or "actors" to mean "people or organisations involved in doing something" rather than "performer on a stage"). Eurospeak may not sound pretty to native English ears, but it may just be a lingua franca forming in front of our eyes. Discardant la textbuch, externalise sus sprachangst y just improviste.

Philip Oltermann, The Guardian, 24 April 2013

Exercises

1. Analyse the cartoon (M 1). A research about the "Euro crisis" will be helpful.
2. Describe the bar chart (M 2) and read the text (M 3). Summarise the findings regarding to "people's trust in Europe" in the 5 countries mentioned.
3. Compare the views and opinions about Germany's/ Merkel's role in the EU (M 4 and M 5).
4. Discuss the pros and cons of Mr Gauck's suggestion to make English the "European language" (M 6) and whether this could help to unite people in Europe.

2.2 Migration

M 7 Headlines

Daily Express
Britain Must Ban Migrants
19 July, 2011

The Sun
Draw a Red Line on Immigration or else
18 December, 2012

Daily Mail
Coalition at War over Migrants
23 December, 2013

Daily Express
We Must Stop the Migrant Invasion
6 June, 2013

Daily Express
Immigration Soars 20% in a Year
26 August, 2011

M 8 Migration in selected European Countries

	Net Migration in European Countries			Foreign Population of EU countries (1 January 2013)		
	2010	2011	2012	Foreign-national	Foreign-born	Total
Belgium	69,268	77,223	72,667	1,253,902	1,747,641	11,161,642
Bulgaria	-	-	-2,512	45,201	96,113	7,284,552
Czech Republic	-12,752	-28,796	-11,769	422,280	387,337	10,516,125
Denmark	10,780	11,240	10,746	374,569	548,411	5,602,628
Germany	151,599	240,377	352,174	7,696,413	10,201,192	82,020,578
Ireland	-25,760	-33,829	-34,997	543,636	736,375	4,591,087
Greece	-915	-15,161	-44,296	862,381	1,235,426	11,062,508
Spain	-42,672	-37,703	-142,553	5,072,680	6,174,740	46,727,890
France	37,580	39,260	39,100	4,089,051	7,537,795	65,578,819
Italy	380,085	303,332	244,556	4,387,721	5,695,883	59,685,227
Netherlands	30,806	25,917	14,135	714,552	1,927,728	16,779,575
Austria	19,327	31,033	39,745	997,038	1,362,185	8,451,149
Poland	-62,995	-108,739	-58,057	58,859	678,946	38,533,299
Portugal	3,815	-24,331	-37,352	417,042	881,440	10,487,289
Romania	-48,100	-47,866	-2,920	70,666	182,939	20,020,074
Sweden	49,948	45,288	51,312	659,374	1,472,353	9,555,893
UK	256,000	205,000	177,000	4,929,710	7,828,376	63,896,077

Oliver Hawkins, House of Commons Library, 17 June, 2014, p. 18 and p. 23

M 9 Polish is second most spoken language in England

Polish has become the most commonly spoken non-native language in England and Wales, it has emerged as figures from the latest Census detail the rise of multicultural Britain.

More than half a million people now speak Polish as their first language, placing it ahead of more established languages Punjabi and Urdu and behind only official languages English and Welsh.

The figures, released today, also show that nearly 140,000 people living in England and Wales cannot speak English, while around 726,000 had a weak grasp of the language. In all, neither English nor Welsh are the main languages for about four million residents, or 8 per cent of the population.

The 2011 Census, which was the first to ask such detailed questions about language in the UK, showed that around 1.6 million could speak the language "well", while around 1.7 million could speak it "very well". It was the main language for 92 per cent of the 50 million residents aged three or older.

Kevin Rawlinson, The Independent, 30 January 2013

M 10 On Shirley Road, can the history of welcoming migrants be lost to Ukip?

Ukip

The UK independence party is a eurosceptic right-wing populist political party in the United Kingdom, founded in 1993.

Wesley Andrews is working his way through a hefty fry-up at the Retro Diner, a no-nonsense cáfe on the Shirley Road in Southampton decorated with union flags, portraits of British bulldogs and images of scooter-riding mods.

His sausage, bacon and eggs go cold as he launches into an attack on the system that he says has turned this street into one of the most ethnically diverse in the UK.

"It's like you're not in Britain," he says. "You can walk up and down this road and not hear anyone speak English. That makes me angry. I know people who've come here, don't work, don't pay taxes but get a big house from the state. I've spoken to people who tell me they're here for the free money."

Andrews and his fellow diners reel off the nicknames for Shirley – Little Poland, Polska, Beirut (the latter not because of the number of Lebanese people here but because it gets a bit rowdy at night).

"And from next year there'll be thousands more here from Romania and Bulgaria. We have poverty in this country and it's getting worse. We're called Great Britain but I don't know what's great about it any more. The government has got to do something about it."

Andrews may be the sort of person politicians of left and right are worrying about as they compete to talk tough on immigration in the wake of Ukip's shock second place in neighbouring Eastleigh's byelection last week.

The rise of Ukip triggered a flurry of anti-Europe stories from the Tory benches and now a series of announcements from Labour this week, culminating in a speech on Thursday by Yvette Cooper, the shadow home secretary, in which she will raise the idea – being discussed in the coalition – of reforming access for new migrants to welfare benefits.

A 28-year-old support worker who cares for people with disabilities, Andrews is from a white Labour-voting family. He is well-educated and well-read. As he speaks, his fellow diners at the Retro nod and grimace. They do not consider him an extremist and he insists he is not a racist: "I've got Polish friends and I look after Asian people at work but it's gone too far. There will be civil unrest, war on the streets."

Across the road, James Morris, 74, an antiques dealer, flies the union flag from his Old Curiosity Shop. He was born around the corner and has seen the street change beyond recognition.

"The whole nature of the place is different. I've worked like a donkey since I was 14 but the immigrants are allowed to come in and get all their bills paid for them," he says. "I don't agree with this idea that Polish people come and do jobs British people won't. I think that's propaganda. A jobless British person would take anything going."

Morris, like many here, has always voted Labour (the party has held Southampton Test since 1997). "But I'm going to take a close look at what Ukip are saying. I'll be listening to those boys carefully before the next general election."

Southampton boasts a long and proud history of immigration over the past 500 years from the Huguenots in the 17th century to the West Indians and Asians in the 20th century. Shirley Road and the High Street are packed with restaurants, shops and supermarkets reflecting that diversity.

Following the enlargement of the EU in 2004, people from eastern Europe, mainly Poland, arrived. The eastern European delicatessens opened, adding to the cultural mix on the Shirley Road.

According to the 2001 census, 89 % of the population in the city were "white British". This had fallen to 78 % by the time of the 2011 census. The "other white" population had increased by more than 200 % to more than 17,000. Today, about a fifth of the city's 237,000-strong population was born outside the UK.

Naturally, not all residents are as strident as Andrews and Morris. Neil Walker, the owner of Retro, is quick to explain that he was not trying to make a political statement by opening a very British-looking café: "It was a business decision. I thought there was a gap in the market for good old staples. Actually I think the Poles and all the other races here have brought good to this area. They've made it more vibrant."

Neil Walker, the owner of the Retro Diner on Shirley Road in Southampton

Quentin Thatcher, an estate agent, agrees: "For us, they've created a demand for housing locally, which has helped our business. They are hard-working, plain-speaking people – good to deal with."

But he is worried about the expected arrival of Romanian and Bulgarian workers. "This is a small island. There is pressure on housing and pressure on services," he says.

Up the road at Southampton general hospital, Sue Smith, a bank worker in her fifties, is waiting to pick up her aunt, who has just been to the eye unit. "You have to wait days to see a doctor now, weeks to get a hospital appointment," she says.

But she also sees good in at least some of her new neighbours. "I've been treated by a Polish doctor and I've got an elderly friend who loves his Polish carer at a nursing home. I don't mind skilled people coming, but there needs to be a way of keeping those without any qualifications away."

The academic studies on British people's reaction to immigration are complicated. According to the latest British Social Attitudes survey from the social research agency NatCen, published at the end of last year, three quarters of people favour "some reduction". This compares with 63 % in 1995 and 72 % in 2003. Just over half say they want a "large" reduction.

Respondents to such surveys are not opposed across the board. Almost 60 % of people say highly skilled migrants from eastern Europe are a positive but this plunges to 19 % for unskilled labourers.

Anna Kopala, 34, one of the first Polish people to arrive after 1994 and the owner of a successful hair salon on Shirley Road, has no time to consider the nuances of such figures. She is too busy. "The world is different," she says. "You can go and work where you want if you have skill and dedication." For her, more people mean more work. "It means more customers for me, more opportunities."

Dorota Zwierzynska, 32, who is a supermarket supervisor and arrived in Hampshire via Dublin and Doncaster, is not so sure the arrival of Romanians and Bulgarians is a good thing. "You read worrying things about them. As long as they work and pay their taxes, that is fine, but I'm concerned they may not."

How does this play out politically? Could the Ukip surge that took place six miles up the road in Eastleigh last week happen here, too?

The Ukip chair in Southampton Test, David Nightingale, a 61-year-old engineer, thinks so. From a standing start with no party machine, he got a respectable 6 % of the votes when he stood in Shirley in last year's city council elections.

Nightingale spent last weekend dropping off leaflets in neighbouring Fareham where he is standing in May as part of Ukip's assault on the Hampshire county council elections. He makes the point in his leaflet that "even" the immigrants are worried about what is happening. [...]

What of the younger generation? Outside Richard Taunton sixth form college, a few minutes walk from Shirley Road, a group of black teenagers bounces a football. "I don't think there's a problem," says one 17-year-old. "A few years ago, it was my parents and grandparents having a tough time. Now it's the Poles who get the stick. I'm not going to say people shouldn't come here."

One of his friends adds: "The EU means we can all go wherever we want, doesn't it? If I can't get a job here when I leave college, I'll go abroad. The world's a big place. You don't have to stay and work where you're born."

Steven Morris, The Guardian, 6 March 2013

Exercises

1. Describe the headlines (M 7). What is the shared message? Can you think of similar headlines in German newspapers?
2. Project: Within the next 4 weeks, collect similar titles or articles of German newspapers and make a collage.
3. Analyse the given table (M 8).
4. Discuss the issue of multiculturalism and native languages as broached in the given report (M 9).
5. Study the newspaper article (M 10) and
   a. List all the people who state their opinion in the given text and present their social background.
   b. Summarise the different views/statements presented in one or two sentences.
   c. TALKSHOW: Choose 5 characters and choose a host for a talk show on the topic: "Immigration from the EU – opportunity or danger for our community" Action!
6. Consider and comment on the challenges that politicians are facing in caring for a multicultural society.

2.3 Britain's role in Europe

M 11 ● Britain to leave the EU?

David Cameron was accused of taking dangerous gamble with Britain's economic future last night, after he bowed to Eurosceptic demands for an in/out referendum on membership of the European Union.
The Prime Minister insisted he was optimistic of winning a "new settlement" for Britain in Europe, saying he wanted to recommend staying in a reformed EU. He promised the British people that they will decide the UK's destiny by the end of 2017 if the Tories win the 2015 general election. But other EU leaders reacted with hostility to his demands and Labour and the Liberal Democrats warned that his gamble could backfire. They said his premature pledge would create five years of uncertainty in which Britain could lose job-creating foreign investment.

Andrew Grice, The Independent, 24 January 2013

M 12 ● The Daily Express campaign

In 2013 the newspaper "Daily Express" started a public campaign promoting Britain's dissociation from the EU.
From now on, our energies will be directed to furthering the cause of those who believe Britain is Better Off Out.
The famous and symbolic Crusader who adorns our masthead will become the figurehead of the struggle to repatriate British sovereignty from a political project that has comprehensively failed people right across Europe.
After far too many years as the victims of Brussels larceny, bullying, over-regulation and all-round interference, the time has come for the British people to win back their country and restore legitimacy and accountability to their political process.
Following the debacle of the Lisbon Treaty – disgracefully imposed upon the public without the referendum they were promised by the three main political parties – many had expected matters European to take a lower profile in British politics.
But the opposite has been true as those on board the European gravy train have mounted one power grab after another. At a time of austerity throughout Europe they have expanded their already bloated budgets, pushing Britain's disproportionate contributions even higher.
And despite not being part of the failing Eurozone, British taxpayers have learned that under Brussels rules agreed to by Labour after it had lost the election they are liable to help bail out economies wrecked by the single currency. A payment of up to £ 10 billion for Ireland is apparently just the start with speculators now starting to target the embattled economy of Portugal. [...]
This newspaper has always been hostile to the dilution of national sovereignty that EU membership entailed, but it has also always acknowledged that economic arguments were key. So long as there was a case to be made that lea-

Daily Express front page, 23 May 2013

ving the EU would risk jobs and investment in Britain there was a powerful brake on thoughts of leaving altogether.

But since the ERM disaster 20 years ago that economic case has utterly collapsed. We were told staying out of the Eurozone would be a financial disaster yet it is now clear beyond doubt that the opposite was true – joining it would have been catastrophic, removing Britain's ability to vary its interest and exchange rates to suit economic circumstances and plunging us into a depression. [...]

While the EU has spread economic sclerosis through its member states the two richest countries in Europe have remained outside: Norway and Switzerland have stayed as the lynch-pins of the European Free Trade Area – able to import from and export to the EU freely without being subjected to its federalist ambitions. Were Britain to break free of Brussels there is no doubt that such a happy status would be open to us. As a heavy net importer from the EU we are simply too important a market for the EU nations to risk cutting ties with.

Taking Britain out of the EU should not be seen as a move to "Little Englandism". On the contrary, ours is a great trading nation with markets all over the world. The time has come to develop our neglected trading links with the new global powerhouses such as China and India.

The creation of the EU is explained by the perfectly understandable desire to avoid further conflict on a continent that had been the scene of two world wars.

But Britain is a land apart: a precious stone set in the silver sea, as Shakespeare so evocatively put it; a realm with a glorious island story stretching back a thousand years, with links to every continent and a language taken up throughout the world.

Our political class bought into the European experiment after losing confidence in our nation and accepting the inevitability of decline. They viewed Europe as a life raft and clambered on board. The British people never took that view.

Now it is Europe that is in decline and Britain that is being held back. It is time to break free.

http://www.express.co.uk/web/europecrusade (10.8.2014)

M 13 ● The other side

Cartoon: Paresh Nath

M 14 Different ideas about Europe

The popular German tabloid Bild recently asked: "Is Britain destroying the EU?" The headline reflects the unease felt across Europe over David Cameron's promise to re-negotiate its EU membership.

Europe now knows what it long suspected: many in Britain have a completely different vision of the EU than those on the continent. David Cameron's European idea is of a flexible, pragmatic union that focuses on trade. The question he asks is: can the EU, as it is currently structured, deliver prosperity? In the rest of Europe they believe that closer integration will build the European dream.

Officials in Brussels said that Cameron was offering a "pick and mix Europe". His vision was for a Europe "à la carte", where countries chose what they liked and disliked. [...]

As regards trying to repatriate powers to Westminster, the President of the European Parliament, Martin Schulz, said it would be a "drawn out and cumbersome negotiation" involving long and complex procedures. The head of the German European Affairs Committee Gunther Krichbaum said the "EU was not a multiple choice event". He compared re-negotiation to "opening Pandora's box".

The German foreign minister went out of his way to say that he hoped the UK would continue to play an "active" and "constructive" role in the EU. He offered a concession: he agreed that not everything decided in Brussels needed to remain at a European level. He signalled that Germany would support some regulations returning to the member states.

Here's the dilemma. There are several states which believe that some measures, currently operated at EU level, could be returned to national governments. Any adjustments, however, they insist must include all 28 members. There is little support for Britain being treated as a special case. The problem for David Cameron is that he is fighting for a complete overhaul of Britain's relationship with Europe, not a tinkering at the edges.

The question I heard asked time and again was what would the prime minister do if he felt he wasn't winning enough concessions. Might he recommend leaving the EU if he didn't get a good deal? A German MP said he thought this negotiation risked "paralysing the EU for years". One German minister was asked about the risk of Britain blackmailing other states to win further opt-outs. He declined to answer. So there is great uncertainty as to what these next years will bring.

One other unknown. It is far from clear whether the German Chancellor, Angela Merkel, will push for a major revision of the treaties in 2015. If she doesn't, that will make Britain's task of re-negotiating far more difficult.

There are divided views in Europe about the referendum. One senior EU official said he welcomed Britain finally deciding whether it wanted to be in or out of Europe. "Let's settle it once and for all," he said. Others said a referendum was "highly risky". Voters might decide to punish the government by voting to leave the EU.

There were lots of statements about how much Europe needs the UK – but not at any price. Some officials welcomed David Cameron's positive remarks about the EU. However, ultimately David Cameron's vision for the EU – a flexible, adaptable union – is not widely shared.

The German foreign minister said: "We do not need less Europe but more integration."

Nothing said can avoid the reality that Britain and much of the EU have very different ideas about the future of the union.

What is clear is that Britain will face a difficult and uphill battle if and when it starts to re-negotiate its membership.

Gavin Hewitt, BBC News, 23 January 2013

M 15 ● Philip, Boris, and Nessie: All provide reasons to stay in EU

Loch Ness in Scotland, home of the famous Loch Ness Monster

Prince Philip, Duke of Edinburgh, born 10 June 1928

Alexander Boris de Pfeffel Johnson, Mayor of London, born 19 June 1964

The Loch Ness Monster has not featured prominently in Britain's debate on its place in Europe, but according to one German newspaper Nessie is one of the main reasons the UK should stay in the EU. "Dear Brits, please stay after all, you're so beautifully crazy," said the tabloid Bild, arguing that eccentric characters such as Prince Philip, Boris Johnson and Sacha Baron Cohen have a lot to offer the Continent.

The article was a rare light note in an otherwise predictably serious Teutonic criticism of David Cameron's UK referendum speech.

On a more thoughtful note the paper applauded the Prime Minister, saying he had bucked a trend that had seen most EU governments agreeing to build Europe without input from their citizens. "It is as if the European project is too important for democracy to have a say," it added.

But DER SPIEGEL labelled Mr Cameron a "scaredy cat", claiming that worries about losing power and influence to Tory right-wingers and Ukip had driven him to make a provocative speech out of fear.

Other commentators from the magazine said it was high time that the rest of Europe stopped trying to keep Britain in the EU. "Travellers on a journey should not be waylaid," wrote columnist Wolfgang Münchau.

The left-of-centre Süddeutsche Zeitung wrote it would be wrong to dismiss outright Mr Cameron's rejection of a bigger Europe, however.

Tony Patterson, The Independent, 24 January 2013

M 16 ● The EU has changed Britain – and mostly for the better

You could argue that it is hard to separate the influence of the EU from the general process of internationalisation that has accompanied improvements in transport and communications. But for a glimpse of how the UK might have developed – or not – without membership of the EU, or the European Economic Community as it was, you might consider Australia as it was 20 years ago, before it reconciled itself culturally to its geography. It was self-absorbed and seemingly content with its lack of ambition, its housing frozen in time and its tasteless English food. Just as we were.

It took Britain's entry into the EU, and the ending of Commonwealth trade ties, to force Australia back on to its own – immensely rich – resources. The same process forced Britain to discover its European self. [...]

Many benefits of EU membership are tangible, and Britain has not been excluded. There is money for infrastructure projects, which – unlike most EU countries – we choose not to announce with grateful placards. And there is the mass of common standards to be met, which make us part of a bloc that has become a global regulatory force. To Eurosceptics this is Brussels "red tape"; we might rather describe it as an entry ticket to civilisation.

But the greatest change for the better from our four decades inside the EU has to do with the country's general outlook. Membership has given the Scots and the Welsh a sense of security that allows them to affirm their national identity in a positive way they were not able to before – an effect that could also be seen in the smaller accession countries. It may eventually do the same for the English. Most of all, though, by exposing Britons to other Europeans and vice versa, it has made us individually, and collectively, more aware of how other Europeans do things, and what we could do better, too.

It has socialised us to an extent many have perhaps not realised. Join the queue to board the Eurostar at St Pancras station, or line up at the easyJet departure lounge at almost any airport in the land, and you will meet a European world, which seems normal and familiar, but would not have been a generation ago.

The difference is not about food or café culture, or the arrival of Zara or Novotel – though the EU has improved our quality of life in all these respects. Nor is it about language per se; Britons retain a foolish pride in their hopelessness at foreign languages. What has changed is our awareness and acceptance of the different European accents and mores. [...] There can be no return to that parochialism. Not only because European consciousness is now lodged inside our heads – yes, even in the head of Nigel Farage – but because our friends and neighbours will do their utmost to prevent it. [...]

Britain's strength, its international influence and its 21st-century identity are perceived by the outside world, above all, as European. That is how others see us. It is also, deep down, how tomorrow's Britons will see themselves.

Mary Dejevsky, The Independent, January 31, 2013

Nigel Farage

British politician and leader of the UK Independence Party, born 3 April 1964

Exercises

1. Describe the given front page. Focus on the crusade logo (M 12).
2. Analyse what the "Daily Express"-crusade is about and why its initiators celebrate a "victory" (M 12).
3. Describe how the British idea of Europe differs from many other member countries (M 12 - 14).
4. Name functions of the media in a democratic system and evaluate this campaign, taking in consideration what type of newspaper the "Daily Express" is (M 12).
5. Analyse the cartoon (M 13).
6. Summarise reasons why Britain should stay in the EU (M 14 - M 16). Use the Internet to find more arguments.
7. Role play:

   Discuss whether Britain should stay in the EU. Take the following sides:

   - Conservative MP who wants Britain to leave the EU
   - Labour MP who wants Britain to stay in the EU
   - Daily Express editor who defends the campaign and its reasons
   - Other journalist who criticises this campaign, its reasons and effects
   - German journalist who takes on a "German view"

3 The European Economy

3.1 The Euro Crisis

M 1 ● A brief history of the Euro Crisis

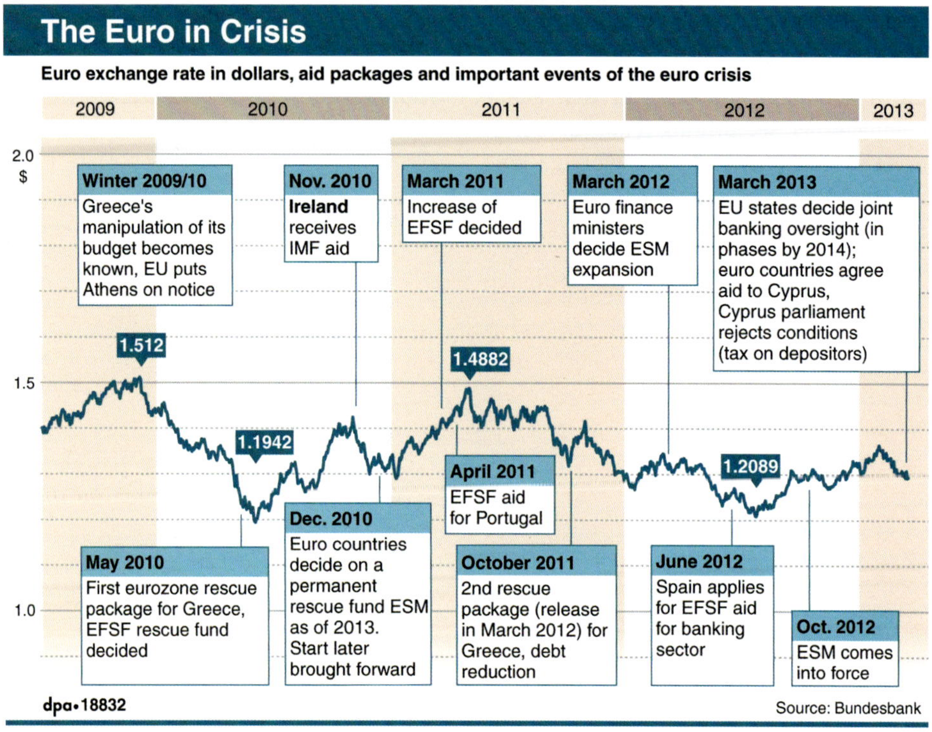

M 2 ● What is the ESM?

The European Stability Mechanism is a new European Union agency that will be able to provide financial assistance to Eurozone countries in difficulty.

It is a permanent agency, based in Luxembourg, and will eventually replace the temporary European Financial Stability Facility (EFSF), although the two will operate in parallel for some time.

How much financial help can it provide?

The ESM will ultimately – from 2014 – be able to use up to 500 bn Euros to help countries in difficulty.

How will the ESM get the money?

It will borrow it from the financial markets, by selling bonds, the same method that governments use for most of their borrowing needs.

Is there a contribution from governments?

The financial foundation of the ESM is capital provided by the Eurozone governments. They have committed a total of 700 bn Euros, although the plan for up to 2014 is that they will actually pay in just 80 bn Euros. The additional capital can be called in if it is needed.

The capital is NOT the money used for providing assistance. It absorbs any losses if countries receiving help fail to repay it. It provides a reassurance to investors in the financial markets that they can lend to the ESM (by buying its bonds) and be confident of being repaid.

Which countries are the biggest contributors?

Germany will provide 27 % of the capital, France 20 % and Italy 18 %.

http://www.bbc.com/news/business-19870747 (12.8.2014)

M 3 ● The situation in Greece in 2012

Sitting in the shade of a mulberry tree in a market square of Volos, Eleni Boubouli is selling dried wild herbs. She picks them herself from the Mount Olympus and other peaks of Thessaly. The simple stall is her way of piecing together a living during Greece's ongoing crisis that includes teaching the odd English lesson, a bit of yoga and some financial support from her retired parents.

"You really need to think about survival now, really think," she says. "Our situation is so bad I don't know how to describe it." Like many Greeks, she feels that the economic maelstrom that has engulfed the country for the past two years will only get worse. A parliamentary election on Sunday, the first since the full onset of the crisis, inspires no confidence that the storm will be calmed.

Rather than wait for the despised political class to improve their lot, Greeks are taking their future into their own hands in ways that involve reversion to the past.

Bartering and exchange schemes that eliminate the Euro are popping up across the country. Farmers are evading supermarkets and selling directly to customers at substantial discounts. And in a reverse of decades of urban migration, there is strong anecdotal evidence that people are leaving Athens in their droves to return to the provinces where they or their parents were raised, to live off the land, find menial work or live without the debts that city life entails.

Ms Boubouli does accept Euros for her produce but also TEM, the Greek acronym for Local Alternative Unit, a coupon scheme that allows members of a network to exchange services and products. Volos, a city on the Aegean coast 200 miles north of Athens, is one of ten such set-ups, with another ten about to start soon.

She recently used 30 TEMs to pay for some legal advice from Elena Dimitriou, a lawyer, who in turn used the coupons for piano lessons, an electrician and food at a weekly market for TEM-friendly producers. "The scheme gives me some protection from this crisis," says Mrs Dimitrou.

"With TEM I can purchase things that I just couldn't afford any more because business is so bad." Another member is Katya Larisaiou, 35, who joined last week and accepts the coupons at the Petit Fleur, a pretty, pastel-coloured café she owns in the town centre.

"Someone said to me that all this bartering is going back 150 years, and I know what he meant. But we have to go backwards to figure out where we should be going," she says, speaking fluent English learnt as a psychology student at the University of Essex. [...]

"I think villages are the future for Greeks the way things are going for our country. You can maintain an acceptable standard of living and Greek nature is fantastic. We have to get back to simple things." Back in the capital, Theodoros Mitropoulos is planning to relocate soon to the village in the Peloponnesian peninsula where he was brought up.

His employment as a carpenter ended two months ago. For the six months before that he was only paid sporadically.

In Greece's boom period before and after the 2004 Olympic Games, he was never out of work and enjoyed a spell of travelling in Europe, outfitting shops.

"Before the issue was how much I liked the job, what I could get out of it," he says. "Now there is no work in Athens, simply none." The bare facts of the crisis brought on by the government's bankcruptcy are staggering: unemployment is at 22 per cent, youth unemployment at 52 per cent; suicides and use of anti-depressants are soaring.

Families' lives are being turned upside down; the normal middle-class expectations of work and wealth accumulation, and the ability to determine one's well-being, have been shattered.

Once resettled in his childhood home, Mr Mitropoulos plans to deliver fish from Patras, a major port, door-to-door in surrounding towns.

"We have some land for animals and growing vegetables. I can use some and sell some. Village life is less expensive, people share things, a café owner doesn't always charge you if he knows you or you've done him a favour. People share." He will leave his wife, a private English teacher whose income has dropped by half, and daughter, a student, in the city. Once his 26-year-old son will have finish military service later in the year, he is likely to join the exodus of young people overseas, to Germany or Britain.

Many middle-aged Greeks fear for their children's future more than theirs.

Amid the rage against the austerity demanded by the second £ 110 billion European rescue loan, there is awareness that the older generations must shoulder some of the blame.

"We all lived off the government directly or indirectly," says Mr Mitropoulos. Voters accepted state largesse without questioning the wisdom or affordability of what was being offered, he thinks, pointing out that his own sister retired at the age of 43 with a full pension – now reduced – of £ 1,500 per month after just 20 years of government service.

"We all expected the state to give and now that has gone because of the bail-out and we have nothing to replace it. That will take a long time."

Alex Spillius, The Telegraph, 3 May 2012

M 4 ● Is the Euro crisis over?

The Eurozone has emerged from recession, borrowing costs have fallen and the risk of Euro area collapse has diminished since mid-2012. However, major causes for concern persist. The economic recovery remains fragile, the currency bloc's politicians are showing a lack of urgency and political uncertainty is rising following the high-profile success of various populist Eurosceptic forces in recent European elections.

Two years ago, with the Eurozone apparently on the brink of collapse and borrowing costs soaring in the bloc's highly-indebted countries, the president of the European Central Bank (ECB), Mario Draghi, made what proved to be two decisive interventions. He pledged to do "whatever it takes" to protect the Euro and announced a new unlimited bond-buying programme [...]. In the period since then, yields on government bonds have plunged in vulnerable countries such as Spain and Italy as investors have returned to the Eurozone sovereign bond markets.

However, this increased demand for government bonds in the Euro area is not fully warranted by the extent of economic recovery. Taken as a whole, the Euro area moved out of recession in mid-2013. But the recovery has been sluggish. A prolonged period of economic stagnation – coupled with sustained low inflation – would make it more difficult for highly indebted households, banks and governments to reduce their debt burdens.

The Euro area's economic outlook remains fragile. Unemployment is high and persistent; governments continue to focus on budget savings; and banks remain reluctant to lend. Against this backdrop, in early June the ECB announced a series of measures aimed at boosting price stability and bolstering the economic recovery, including cuts to the main interest rates and the provision of cheap funding to banks.

On the positive side, some of the short-term pain that the Eurozone's weaker economies have endured is likely to deliver lasting benefits. Structural reforms and austerity measures that have been passed across the Euro area should support private sector activity in the medium term. The average cost of labour per unit of output has fallen significantly in the likes of Greece, Portugal and Spain. This has boosted companies' competitiveness and external trade balances in the vulnerable countries. Regulatory reform has improved the business environment, for example, by increasing labour-market flexibility, boosting investment incentives and opening closed professions. But the political and socio-economic costs of these reforms remain a source of concern. In particular, youth unemployment has reached crisis proportions and risks producing a "lost generation" of individuals with little work experience and limited employability. This is not just a personal tragedy, but also threatens to undermine long-term growth prospects. [...]

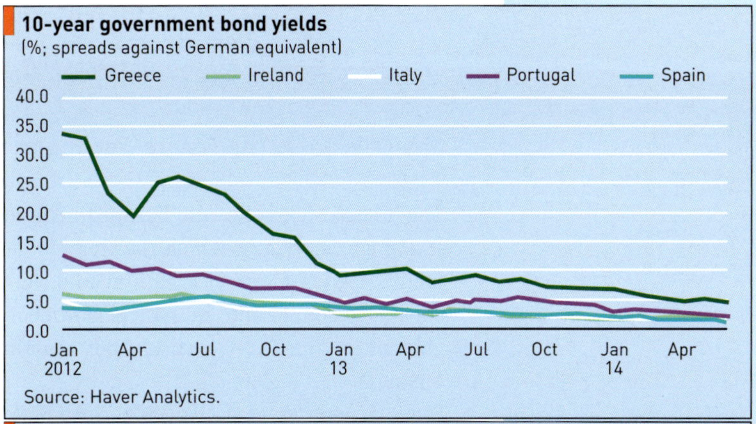

10-year government bond yields
(%; spreads against German equivalent)
Source: Haver Analytics.

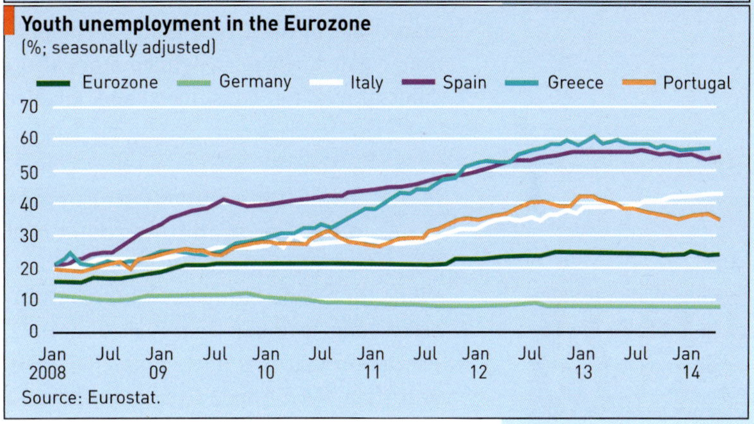

Youth unemployment in the Eurozone
(%; seasonally adjusted)
Source: Eurostat.

Meanwhile, the health of banks remains fragile. [...] Finally, some of the sense of security that followed decisive ECB rhetoric two years ago has proved to be false. In particular, the currency bloc's politicians are showing a lack of urgency as they struggle to put the Euro area on a more sustainable institutional footing. [...]

Without a viable banking union, financial instability and debt crises are likely to return to the Eurozone in the medium to long term.

Martin Koehring, From The Economist Intelligence Unit, 24 July 2014

Exercises

1. Analyse the chart (M1).
2. Explain how the ESFS and ESM institutions work (M 2).
3. What effects does the financial crisis in Greece have on the daily lives of the citizens (M3)?
4. Is the Euro crisis over? Comment on this question (M 4).

3.2 The Single European Market – a never ending story?

M 5 ● What is the Single European Market?

The internal market of the European Union is a single market in which the free movement of goods, services, capital and persons is ensured and in which European citizens are free to live, work, study and do business.

Since it was created in 1993, the single market has opened itself more to competition, created new jobs, defined more affordable prices for consumers and enabled businesses and citizens to benefit from a wide choice of goods and services.

The European Union is working towards further simplification of the regulations which still prevent citizens and businesses from making the most of the advantages of the single market.

http://eus-lex.europa.eu, © Eropäische Union, 1998 – 2014

M 6 ● The Single European Payments Area (SEPA) – a further step towards completion?

While the Single European Market advanced a long way between 1987 and 1992, the notion that it is now complete is hard to sustain, even from a legal point of view. The Single Euro Payments Area (SEPA) creates a true European Single Market for retail payments in Euro where transfers, direct debits and payments between Member States are as easy and fast as the equivalent domestic transactions. It will become fully operational in all Eurozone countries on 1st August 2014. It will also apply to Euro-denominated transactions in non-Eurozone countries from 30th October 2016. SEPA will greatly facilitate Euro payments for citizens and businesses and increase competition between banks.

What is the "Single Euro Payments Area" (SEPA)?

The introduction of the Euro has helped to make a cash payment anywhere in the Euro area just as easy as at home. But until recently it was not so easy to pay for goods or services electronically in another Euro area country, for example with your bank debit card – a means of payment favoured by many Europeans today. And if you wanted to transfer money from your home bank account to an account in another Euro area country, the payment could take much longer, and sometimes the beneficiary did not get the full amount.

The Single Euro Payments Area (or "SEPA" for short) changes all this. It makes all electronic payments in the Euro area as easy as cash payments. You can make fast and secure transfers between bank accounts anywhere in the Euro area. And if you are shopping abroad, you can also use your bank debit card to make a payment in Euro, as you would in your home country. SEPA is where more than 500 million citizens, over 20 million businesses and European public authorities can make and receive payments in Euro under the same basic conditions, rights and obligations, regardless of their location.

It also means better banking services for all: transparent pricing, valuable guarantees ensuring that your payments are received promptly and in full, and banks assuming responsibility if something goes wrong with your payment.

http://europa.eu/rapid/press-release_MEMO-14-502_en.htm?locale=en (20.8.2014)

M 7 ● Europe opens trade talks with US

The Transatlantic Trade and Investment Partnership (TTIP) is a trade agreement that is presently being negotiated between the European Union and the United States. It aims at removing trade barriers in a wide range of economic sectors to make it easier to buy and sell goods and services between the EU and the US.

On top of cutting tariffs across all sectors, the EU and the US want to tackle barriers behind the customs border – such as differences in technical regulations, standards and approval procedures. These often cost unnecessary time and money to companies who want to sell their products in both markets. For example, when a car is approved as safe in the EU, it has to undergo a new approval procedure in the US even though their safety standards are similar.

The TTIP negotiations will also look at opening both markets for services, investment, and public procurement. They could also shape global rules on trade. Talks started in July 2013.

http://ec.europa.eu/trade/policy/in-focus/ttip/about-ttip/ (12.9.2014)

TTIP is said to boost

- the EU's economy by € 120 billion;
- the US's economy by € 90 billion;
- the rest of the world's economy by € 100 billion.

The deal would cover about 50 % of the global economic output and 30 % of global trade and because of its magnitude it would create de facto global standards.

Source: European Union, 2014

Exercises

1. Name the four types of freedom that are ensured by the agreement of the European internal market (M 5).
2. Draw a chart presenting the benefits mentioned in the text and think of other benefits, as well as potential dangers, that come with this agreement (M 6).
3. Explain why the introduction of SEPA was a necessary "next step" in order to complete the idea of the European internal market (M 6).
4. Group work/Internet research/presentations:
   Educational programmes and projects implemented by the EU have become more and more important when it comes to European education. Find examples of such programmes and projects and tell the class how you can benefit from them.
5. After reading M 7 and gathering more information at home about the TTIP – its plans and negotiations, lead a fishbowl discussion about the pros and cons of the TTIP for the European consumers.

4 Europe's future – Nationalism vs European identity?

M 1 Scotland votes to remain part of United Kingdom

In many member countries of the EU there are regions people would like to see (more) independent from the rest of the country and its government. Examples are the Scottish, who had a referendum on September 18th, 2014, where voters were asked if they wanted Scotland to stay in the UK or live in an independent Scotland. Other countries where we can find such movements are e.g. Belgium, Italy, France and Spain.

The day of the most important popular vote in Scottish history began with a buzz of excitement on the streets of this ancient capital. "Yes" signs filled city windows, Scottish flags flew from car antennas, and kilts added a rainbow of tartan to many gray, cobbled streets.

Voters discussing in the streets of Edinburgh after having cast their ballot on Scottish independence.

For supporters of independence, a 307-year-old goal of sovereignty appeared finally, tantalizingly, within their grasp.

But for all their hopes, all the late momentum they seemed to seize, the day belonged to a quiet, unswayed swath of Scots who brought to the ballot box a conviction that the United Kingdom, in the "No" camp's words, is better together.

"It was too big of a risk," said Laura McGill, a 26-year-old emigrant from Australia who works in a law firm. "I didn't feel some questions were answered sufficiently."

McGill was concerned that the nationalists did not have a plan for a new Scottish currency if the British pound was not an option, as London had warned it would not be. She also questioned whether the new country's revenues would be sufficient to pay its share of the United Kingdom's debt. What would happen if they weren't?

Many Scots apparently shared her fears. Going it alone, for all its emotional appeal, seemed fraught with too much uncertainty.

The result was disappointing and sometimes devastating to "Yes" supporters. Poll after poll had showed a steady climb in their numbers until the race, by consensus, had become too close to call when voting stations opened at 7 a.m. Thursday.

"Yes" owned the streets throughout the day, with supporters knocking on doors, filling the pubs to watch the results, and marching gleefully up and down the Royal Mile with banners waving and voices raised in song.

"We want to be part of the world stage and have a direct line to talk with the rest of the world," said Andrew McIlvride, who traveled to Edinburgh from Argyll, in the Highlands, to be part of history. "This would mean an absolute revisiting of our self-pride and sense of nation."

It was not to be.

At Greenmantle, a pub filled to capacity near Edinburgh University, what had been a raucous, confident, pro-independence crowd grew restless, then quiet, and finally dispirited as the results trickled in.

First to announce was Clackmannanshire, between the urban centers of Edinburgh and Glasgow, where the "No" campaign won by a margin of 54 to 46 percent. Then the Orkney Islands, north of the Scottish mainland, trounced the "Yes" movement by more than 2 to 1.

"That's a worry for me," Rory Penman said as he pondered the data. "That would be so Scottish, to vote against your own independence."

The news got worse as the night wore on, and what had been a laughing, engaged, shoulder-to-shoulder crowd began to collect their belongings about 2 a.m. and head disconsolately into a cold mist.

Some voters saw hope in a national discussion that lasted for more than two years and attracted an astonishing number of people to the polls.

"People are wanting change, whether they're voting yes or no," said Euan Dickson, a 20-year-old university student who voted for independence.

The Conservative government in London apparently agrees, having pledged before the vote to grant Scotland more authority whatever the outcome of the referendum.

In the end, however, the camp that had been much less vocal, much less visible, and much more concerned about the security of their families and country chose the status quo.

As a result, the United Kingdom will remain together, the Union Jack will continue to fly, and these often-fractious neighbors will try to adjust to a shaken and changed relationship.

Brian MacQuarrie, The Boston Globe, 19 September 2014

M 2 ● The pros and cons of Scottish independence

1. Decisions about Scotland are best made by the people who live here	1. The UK is a successful union dating back 300 years
2. Scotland can be a successful country in its own right	2. Being part of the UK offers more economic security
3. An independent Scotland would make decisions that reflect Scottish priorities	3. Jobs could be lost
4. Independence would be a declaration of confidence in ourselves and our nation	4. Major projects could be frozen
5. Scotland could set its own welfare priorities	5. Prices could rise
6. Scotland could get rid of nuclear weapons from Scottish soil	6. Scotland benefits from UK research funding
7. Scotland would not get dragged into illegal wars	7. No-one knows what currency Scotland would use
8. North Sea oil revenues would be put to good use	8. Scotland would have less influence in the world
9. Scotland could adopt a different immigration policy, because Scotland needs an increase in the working population	9. The BBC should not be put at risk
10. Scotland will continue to have good relationships with England, Wales and Northern Ireland but on a more equal basis	10. Security is better handled on a UK-wide basis

French philosopher André Glucksmann, born 19 June 1939

M 3 Europe is still a playground of ideas

French philosopher André Glucksmann finds the situation in Europe "extremely unsettling." In a SPIEGEL interview, he discusses the failure of European intellectuals, how divisions could lead to an EU breakup or even hostilities, and why pursuing a United States of Europe is "the wrong goal."

SPIEGEL: Mr. Glucksmann, in light of the intellectual and existential experiences you had in the 20th century as an anti-totalitarian thinker, are you worried about Europe's future?

Glucksmann: I've never believed that all the dangers were averted after the end of fascism and communism. History doesn't come to a standstill. Europe didn't step out of (history) when the Iron Curtain disappeared, even if it has occasionally seemed to want to. Democracies tend to ignore or forget the tragic dimensions of history. In this sense, I would say: Yes, current developments are extremely unsettling.

SPIEGEL: Since its beginnings 60 years ago, the European community has almost always stumbled from one crisis to the next. Setbacks are part of its normal mode of operation.

Glucksmann: A sense of crisis characterizes the modern European era. From it, one can draw the general conclusion that Europe actually isn't a state or a community in the national sense, which grows together organically. It also can't be compared with the ancient Greek city-states, which, despite their differences and rivalries, formed a single cultural unit.

SPIEGEL: European countries are also bound by shared cultural aspects. Is there such a thing as a European spirit?

Glucksmann: European nations are not alike, which is why they can't be merged together. What unites them is not a community but a societal model. There is a European civilization and a Western way of thinking.

SPIEGEL: What are its features?

Glucksmann: Since the Greeks – from Socrates to Plato to Aristotle – Western philosophy has inherited two fundamental principles: Man is not the measure of all things, and he isn't immune to failure and evil. Nevertheless, he is responsible for himself, and for everything he does or refrains from doing. The adventure of mankind is an uninterrupted human creation. God is not part of it.

SPIEGEL: Fallibility and freedom. But are these fundamental aspects of European intellectual history not enough to create a permanent political union?

Glucksmann: Europe was never a national entity, not even in the Christian Middle Ages. Christianity always remained divided – the Romans, the Greeks and later the Protestants. A European federal state or European confederation is a distant goal that is frozen in the abstraction of the term. I think pursuing it is the wrong goal.

SPIEGEL: Is the European Union chasing after a utopia in both political and historical terms?

Glucksmann: The EU's founding fathers liked to invoke the Carolingian myth, and an EU award was named after Charlemagne. But, after all, his grandchildren divided up his empire. Europe is a unity in its division or a division in its unity. Whichever way you put it, though, it's clearly not a community in terms of religion, language or morals.

SPIEGEL: And yet it exists. What does that lead you to conclude?

Glucksmann: The crisis of the European Union is a symptom of its civilization. It doesn't define itself based on its identity but, rather, on its otherness. A civilization isn't necessarily based on a common desire to achieve the best but, rather, on excluding and making the evil taboo. In historical terms, the European Union is a defensive reaction to horror.

SPIEGEL: A negatively defined entity that

emerged out of the experience of two world wars?

Glucksmann: In the Middle Ages, the faithful prayed and sang in their litanies: "Lord, protect us from pestilence, hunger and war." This means that community exists not for good but against evil.

SPIEGEL: These days, many people cite the phrase "never another war" as Europe's raison d'être. Does this foundation still hold up now that the specter of war in Europe has dissipated?

Glucksmann: The Balkan wars in the former Yugoslavia and the murderous incendiary actions of the Russians in the Caucasus didn't happen that long ago. The European Union came together to oppose three evils: the memory of Hitler, the Holocaust, racism and extreme nationalism; Soviet communism in the Cold War; and, finally, colonialism, which some countries in the European community had to painfully abandon. These three evils gave rise to a common understanding of democracy, a civilizing central theme of Europe.

SPIEGEL: Is a new, unifying challenge what's missing today?

Glucksmann: It wouldn't be hard to find if Europe didn't act so heedlessly. In the early 1950s, the core of the union was the establishment of the European Coal and Steel Community (ECSC), the first supranational economic alliance in the area of heavy industry; (it was) Lorraine and the Ruhr area, the ECSC as a means of preventing war. The counterpart today would be a European energy union. Instead, Germany decided to embark on its transition to renewable energy on its own, ignoring the European dimension. Everyone is negotiating individually with Russia for oil and gas, Germany signed an agreement to build the Baltic Sea pipeline despite the resistance of Poland and Ukraine, and Italy is involved in the South Stream pipeline through the Black Sea.

SPIEGEL: So each country is pursuing its own interests amid changing alliances and bilateral agreements that ignore the spirit of the European Union?

Glucksmann: (This is a) grim example of cacophony because it shows that the member states are no longer willing and able to form a united front against external threats and Europe's challenges in the globalized world. This touches on the nerve of the European civilization project, in which each person is supposed to be able to live for himself, and with which, however, everyone wants to survive together. And it makes things easy for Russia under (President Vladimir) Putin. Despite all the weakness of that giant of natural resources, its capacity to cause damage remains considerable and is something its president likes to use. Recklessness and forgetfulness create the conditions for new catastrophes in both the economy and politics. [...]

SPIEGEL: The EU hasn't lost its appeal. No one is voluntarily leaving the Eurozone.

Glucksmann: Socrates said that no one willingly does wrong. I interpret this as follows: Bad things happen when the will grows weak. It doesn't seem to me that finding solutions and paths in the current financial crisis is a superhuman task. After all, the EU's leaders keep finding them here and there.

SPIEGEL: And they're finding their way from one Brussels summit to the next, and at increasingly shorter intervals. But what are supposed to be solutions just don't pan out.

Glucksmann: What's missing is a global perspective. The why of the European Union, its raison d'être, has been lost. There will always be ways to improve the EU institutions and adjust them to the needs of the situation. We can rely on the resourcefulness of politicians and lawyers to do this. The challenge appears at a different level, and it's clearly a matter of survival: If the old European nations don't unite and present a unified front, they will perish.

SPIEGEL: But haven't European leaders recognized this?

Glucksmann: If they have, why are they acting with so little unity? The question of size has become an absolute necessity in globalization. Mrs. Merkel undoubtedly senses that Germany's fate will also be decided in Europe's backyard. That's why, after some hesitation, she chose solidarity, albeit in moderation. Nevertheless, she is also allowing Germany, France, Italy and Spain to become divided in the crisis. If our countries can become divided under the pressure of market forces, they will perish, both individually and jointly.

SPIEGEL: Are you saying that the idea of a European community of fate hasn't really taken hold yet?

Glucksmann: Not in practice. Globalization brings global chaos, and a global police force – which the United States played for a long time – no longer exists. The players may not be keen on war, but they don't exactly mean well by one another. Everyone is playing his own game. In this anarchic confusion, Europe has to assert itself and face up to threats offensively. Putin's Russia, which wants to regain parts of what it lost, is a threat. China, a bureaucratic slave state, is a threat. Militant Islamism is a threat. Europe has to learn to think in terms of hostility once again. [...]

SPIEGEL: For many parts of the world, Europe is a beacon of freedom and human rights.

Glucksmann: But ideals and values don't combine to form prospects. European nations can certainly have an attractive pluralism of values, but presenting them as if they were part of a catalog isn't sufficient. Instead, it's important to address the challenges together. [...] The great universal historian Arnold J. Toynbee evaluated the development of cultures on the basis of their ability to appropriately react to challenges. Is Europe willing to confront its fate? There is reason to doubt it.

SPIEGEL: Does this result from a lack of leadership?

Glucksmann: It's more than that. It's also a question of the failure of intellectuals, indifference in public opinion and isolationism. Look at the elections in Europe. What role do foreign policy and Europe's place in the world play? [...] The 21st century will be the century of big continents that will either get along with each other or not. If Europe doesn't enter this dimension, it will fall back into the 19th century. Then our political activity will only be based on distant memories: Europe, the continent of anguish and nostalgia.

Interview conducted by Romain Leick, Spiegel Online International, 23 August 2012, Transaltion: Christopher Sultan

Exercises

1. Explain why a majority of the Scottish people finally voted to remain part of the UK (M 1).
2. Should Scotland have voted for independence? Comment on this question (M 1, M 2).
3. Find out more about independence movements in other European countries and examine their main motives.
4. Summarise Mr Glucksmann's vision of Europe's future (M 3).
5. Have a final discussion in your class: Which way will Europe go? To an increasingly federalised system or back to a more nation-centered power? Which option is best in your opinion?

Seite 7

(to) wither by the wayside	am Wegesrand vertrocknen
(to) espouse	hier: unterstützen
due course	zu gegebener Zeit
comity of nations	gutes Einvernehmen der Völker
overweening	anmaßend

Seite 8

sublime	das Erhabene, Noble

Seite 12

(to) unleash s.o./s.th	jmd./etw. entfesseln, freisetzen
hubris	Überheblichkeit, Anmaßung (Hybris)
(to) pledge	versprechen, verpflichten

Seite 15

raft	hier: Menge
(to) tout s.th.	etwas (aufdringlich) ankündigen, anpreisen

Seite 17

(to) wrench	zerren, reißen
bailout	Rettungsaktion
vertiginous	schwindelerregend
(to) underpin	stärken, stützen, untermauern
in the runup to s.th.	im Vorfeld von etw.

Seite 18

(to) quip	spötteln, witzeln

Seite 22

no-nonsense (Adj.)	geradlinig
(to) reel off	hier: herunterspulen, aufzählen

Seite 23

strident	scharf, schrill
staple	hier: Hausmannskost

Seite 24

surge	Zunahme, plötzlicher Erfolg

Seite 25

(to) adorn	schmücken, zieren
masthead	hier: Titel, Zeitungskopf
figurehead	Galionsfigur, Aushängeschild
larceny	Diebstahl
dilution	Verwässerung, Verdünnung

Seite 26

lynchpin	Dreh- und Angelpunkt, Stütze

Seite 27

cumbersome	beschwerlich, lästig, mühsam
(to) tinker s.th.	etwas flicken

Seite 28

(to) waylay	hier: aufhalten, eigentlich: auflauern, wegelagern

Seite 30

bonds	Anleihen

Seite 31

stall	Marktstand, Bude
maelstrom	Mahlstrom, Sog, Wirbel
bartering	Tauschhandel

Seite 32

spell	Weile, Dauer
yield	Rendite, Gewinne, hier: Zinsen
(to) plunge	einbrechen, stürzen
sluggish	träge, schwerfällig

Seite 34

austerity measures	Sparmaßnahmen

Seite 36

tartan	karierter Schottenstoff
cobbled	gepflastert
unswayed	unbeeinflusst
swath	breiter (Mäh-)Streifen
raucous	lärmend, laut

Seite 39

litany	Litanei, Gebetgesang
raison d'être (franz.)	Existenz-, Daseinsberechtigung
specter	Phantom, Schreckgespenst
incendiary	brandstiftend
heedless	achtlos, rücksichtslos
cacophony	Kakophonie, Missklang
not to pan out	nicht gut laufen

1. Agreeing

I agree with ...
I couldn't agree more ...
You're absolutely right there ...
I can see your point ...
You're right up to a point ...
Exactly ...
I can understand ...

2. Disagreeing

You're missing the point ...
I totally disagree with ...
That's all very well, but ...
You may not believe it, but
I can't accept ...
Wouldn't it be better to ...
I see what you mean, but
I see your point, but I think ...
Yes, but on the other hand ...
I'm not with you there ...
What I object to is ...
I (very much) doubt whether ...
That can't be right!
Never!

3. Clarifying

Absolutely right, but ...
Let us focus on this issue here ...
What has that got to do with ...
Have you thought of ...
Let me give you another example ...
I don't see what you mean ...
You must admit that ...
Do you realize ...
What do you mean by ...
So you are saying that ...
The main priority is ...
Why do you say that ...
Well, it depends on ...
Is there any reason why ...
Do you really mean to say that ...
Let me put this clear ...
It may sound strange but ...

4. Giving an opinion

My feeling is ...
What I'm concerned with is ...
I hold the view that ...
If you ask me ...
An additional argument I would like to present is that ...
I'm pretty sure that ...
My personal view is that ...
In my experience ...
Personally, I think/believe/suppose ...
The surprising thing is that ...
I'm fairly certain that ...
I'm convinced that ...
To my mind ...
In my opinion/ I'm of the opinion ...
The fact of the matter is ...
It is my firm believe that ...
The way I see it ...

5. Giving in

What I like about this argument/thought is ...
I take that back ...
There is some common ground between us here ...
I think we can draw the following conclusion ...
I have never thought of/about that before ...
I see things in a different light now ...
I can see your point ...
I must admit that ...

6. Interrupting

I'm sorry, but ...
Excuse me, can/may I add something?
Sorry to interrupt, but ...
Just listen for a moment ...
I am trying to answer your question ...
As I have said it before ...
Do you mind if I jump in here?
Pardon me ...
I don't mean to intrude ...

PICTURE CREDITS

Belltoons / © Steve Bell 2012, East Sussex – S. 16

Cagle Cartoons / Paresh Nath, Santa Barbara – S. 26

Daily Express, 23. Mai 2013 – S. 25

dpa Infografik, Frankfurt – S. 5, 30

dpa Picture Alliance / Yunus Kaymaz, Frankfurt – S. 36

Getty Images / Getty Images News / Getty Images Europe, München – S. 38; / Popperfoto – S. 7

hgm-press, Berlin – S. 23

Oliver Schuck / toonpool.com, Berlin – S. 17

Thinkstock / iStockphoto – Einband (3), 34; / iStockphoto / Ruskpp – S. 35

ullstein bild / Roger Viollet, Berlin – S. 7

© VG Bild-Kunst, Bonn 2015 – S. 10

Wikipedia / Bundesarchiv, B 145 Bild-F004665-0003 / Unterberg, Rolf / CC-BY-SA – S. 7; Bundesarchiv, Bild 183-19000-2453 / CC-BY-SA – S. 7; / Foto-AG Gymnasium Melle / CC-BY-3.0 – S. 14; / Howcheng – S. 7; / Sam Fentress / CC-BY-SA-2.0 – S. 28; / johnhemming / CC-BY-SA-2.0 – S. 28; / Michael Lucan / CC-BY-3.0 – S. 12; / Jamie McCaffrey / CC-BY-2.0 – S. 28; / OgreBot – S. 7